PINCH OF TIME

Meals in Less than 30 Minutes

Sandra Rudloff

BRISTOL PUBLISHING ENTERPRISES
San Leandro, California

A **nitty gritty**® Cookbook

Printed in the United States of America.

ISBN: 1-55867-251-6

Cover design: Frank J. Paredes
Cover photography: John A. Benson
Food stylist: Susan De Vaty
Illustrations: Grant Corley

CONTENTS

PINCH OF TIME

Especially on workdays or our busiest days, we feel the pinch of time. Thirty minutes or less is quite often all the time we have to make a meal. You can make fresh meals in that amount of time, without the use of instant mixes, frozen foods, or even the microwave. The key is in how you use the 30 minutes that you have.

A key component of cooking in a small amount of time is to use that time to your advantage. **While one thing is cooking, use that time to chop up the next ingredient**. Or while your meat is browning, begin cooking the sauce in another pot, and in turn, reduce the time it takes to do the whole recipe. *Mise en place* — everything in place before you begin cooking – is how you're taught in cooking schools, but it's not always practical.

Keep basic ingredients handy, and be prepared to **substitute** ingredients. Shopping is very time-consuming. Plan your shopping wisely, and try to be flexible about making ingredient substitutions: you'll have more time in the kitchen, and feel more in control of your menus.

Smaller pieces. There is really no way to reduce the amount of time it takes to roast a large chunk of beef. But cutting that chunk into smaller pieces will speed things up.

The right equipment also helps a lot. I recommend a good nonstick skillet and pots.

Finally, **use ingredients that are packaged for convenience**. Packaged, prewashed lettuce saves a lot of preparation time. Many stores also sell fresh vegetables already cut and cleaned, or chicken that has already been cut and marinated. Use them!

The recipes in this book have all been tested and timed, and can be ready to serve in 30 minutes or less.

SOUPS AND SALADS

ITALIAN BEAN SOUP

It's a meal in a pot; all you need is the fresh bread to accompany it.

1/2 lb. Italian sausage
2 tbs. olive oil
1/2 chopped cup yellow onion
1 carrot, chopped
1 zucchini, chopped
2 cans (15 oz. each) cannellini beans, rinsed and drained
2 cans (14 1/2 oz. each) chicken broth
grated Parmesan cheese

In a Dutch oven or large pot, brown sausages over medium-high heat. When brown, remove from pot and set aside to cool. Drain off any fat in pot. Add oil and onion. Cook until translucent. Add carrot, zucchini, beans and broth. Increase heat to high and bring to a boil.

Cut sausages into 1/4-inch thick slices and add to soup. Cover and simmer until vegetables are tender, about 15 minutes. Pass cheese to sprinkle on top, if desired.

BLACK BEAN SOUP

Servings: 6

You don't have to soak beans all night and cook them all day to get a rich, thick soup. This soup is a super time-saver, because after you combine all the ingredients, you only need to stir occasionally.

1 can (16 oz.) refried black beans
1 can (14.5 oz.) chicken broth*
3 cans (16 oz. each) black beans, undrained
1 russet potato, minced
1 cup corn kernels, frozen or canned

$\frac{1}{2}$ yellow onion, minced
$1\frac{1}{2}$ tsp. ground cumin
$\frac{1}{4}$ tsp. cayenne pepper
$\frac{3}{4}$ tsp. salt
2 tbs. Worcestershire sauce

In a large pot, combine refried beans and broth; stir to mix and break up beans. Add all remaining ingredients and bring mixture to a boil, stirring frequently. Cover and reduce heat to medium-low, stirring occasionally. Simmer for 15 to 20 minutes, or until potatoes are tender.

*This makes a very thick soup. If you prefer a thinner soup, add chicken broth or water, $\frac{1}{4}$ cupfuls at a time, until you reach the desired consistency.

SPRING VEGETABLE SOUP

Servings: 4-6

Be sure to not overcook this soup, as you want to show the bright colors of the vegetables. Look for the tiniest potatoes you can find.

6 cups chicken broth
2 cups chopped cooked chicken
$1/2$ lb. baby new potatoes
$1/2$ lb. fresh asparagus
$1/2$ lb. sugar snap peas
$1/2$ lb. baby yellow zucchini

In a large soup pot, heat broth, chicken meat and potatoes to a full boil. Reduce heat to medium and cook for about 5 minutes, or until potatoes are just tender.

Cut asparagus diagonally into $1/4$-inch thick slices. Trim ends of the peas and baby zucchini. Add zucchini to pot and cook for 5 minutes. Add asparagus and peas. Cook until tender-crisp and serve immediately.

CARROT AND SQUASH SOUP

These vegetables are available year round, but I tend to think of this as a fall or winter soup. With some crusty bread, it makes a light meal.

1 lb. carrots
1 lb. banana squash
6 cups chicken broth
1 1/4 tsp. curry powder
1/4 tsp. cayenne pepper
1 tsp. salt

Peel and cut carrots into 1/2-inch pieces. Peel and seed banana squash and cut into 1-inch pieces. Place all ingredients in a large saucepan or soup pot. Bring mixture to a boil over high heat; reduce heat to medium-low, cover and simmer for about 20 minutes, or until carrots and squash are very tender.

Place a portion of the soup in a blender and pulse until smooth. Continue until all soup has been pureed. Taste, correct seasoning if needed, and serve.

HOT AND SOUR SOUP

It is actually faster to make your own hot and sour soup than ordering it in from a restaurant. If you are brave, or want more heat, just increase the amount of red peppers you put in.

2 cans (14.5 oz. each) beef broth
1/4 cup sherry
1 tbs. soy sauce
1/2 tsp. crushed red peppers
1 tsp. cornstarch
1 egg

2/3 cup tofu, cut into 1/2-inch cubes
1/3 cup slivered bamboo shoots
1/4 cup slivered green onions
3 tbs. white vinegar
2/3 cup cooked shrimp or chicken,
     optional

In a large saucepan or soup pot, combine broth, sherry, soy sauce, peppers and cornstarch. Stir well to combine. Bring mixture to a boil over high heat, stirring frequently. Reduce heat to medium and continue to boil to reduce and thicken broth. Cook for 15 minutes at a continuous boil.

Beat egg in a small bowl. Add egg to boiling broth, stirring slowly while adding. Add all remaining ingredients and bring to a full boil. Serve immediately.

SOUPS AND SALADS   7

CREAMY CRAB SOUP

Servings: 4-6

This very elegant soup can also be served as an appetizer.

6 cups chicken broth
¼ cup sherry
1 russet potato, peeled and diced
½ tsp. salt
1 lb. lump crabmeat
1 cup heavy cream

In a large pot, combine broth, sherry and potato. Bring to a boil over high heat. Reduce heat to medium, cover and simmer until potatoes are tender, about 15 minutes.

Remove potatoes from broth and place in a blender (use a bit of broth if needed.) Pulse until smooth. Return puree to broth, and add salt and crabmeat. Bring soup to a boil, remove from heat and stir in cream. Serve immediately.

SALMON AND WILD RICE SOUP

I usually don't like to use mixes, but utilizing a packaged long-grain and wild rice mix gives this soup perfect seasoning, and ease of finding all the ingredients in the amount you need. I prefer to use rice mixes made with converted rice, so the grains hold up better in the soup without turning mushy.

3½ cups water
1 can (14 oz.) chicken or vegetable broth
1 pkg. (6 oz.) long-grain and wild rice mix
½ cup chopped yellow onion
2 stalks celery, thinly sliced

4 oz. fresh mushrooms, sliced
½ tsp. salt
1 boneless, skinless salmon fillet,
    about 8 oz.
1 cup half-and-half

In a large soup pot, combine water, broth, rice, onion, celery, mushrooms and salt. Bring mixture to a boil over high heat. Reduce heat to medium-low, cover and simmer for 15 minutes.

While soup is cooking, cut salmon into very small pieces. Add salmon and increase heat to high to return soup to a full boil. Reduce heat to low, cover and simmer for an additional 5 minutes. Remove from heat and add half-and-half, stirring well to mix. Serve immediately.

WHITE BEAN AND PANCETTA SALAD

Pancetta is a cured Italian bacon, and accents this bean salad wonderfully. It is a rustic Italian dish that goes well with a glass of cold wine.

1 cup finely chopped pancetta
2 cans (15 oz. each) cannellini beans (white beans), rinsed and drained
½ red onion, chopped
1 cup chopped fresh tomatoes
¼ cup chopped fresh Italian parsley
1 clove garlic, minced or pressed
½ cup olive oil
¼ cup red wine vinegar
4 cups baby lettuce leaves

In a small skillet, sauté pancetta over medium-high heat until fat is rendered out, about 5 minutes. Remove from skillet and drain on paper towels. Let cool.

In a medium bowl, combine all ingredients except lettuce. Stir to mix well. Place lettuce in a serving bowl and top with bean salad.

CHOPPED CLUB SALAD

This salad features bite-sized pieces of everything you love in a clubhouse sandwich. The key here is to try and make everything the same size — aim for pieces about the size of a nickel.

1/2 cup mayonnaise
3 tbs. vinegar
1 tsp. salt
4 hard-cooked eggs, chopped
12 cups chopped iceberg lettuce
12 slices bacon, cooked crisp and chopped
12 oz. sliced smoked turkey, chopped
1/2 cup chopped red onion
1 1/2 cups chopped fresh tomato

In a small bowl, mix together mayonnaise, vinegar and salt. Combine all ingredients, including mayonnaise mixture, in a large bowl, and toss to coat. Serve immediately.

SOUPS AND SALADS   11

AVOCADO AND APPLE SALAD WITH CHICKEN

Servings: 4

I love this salad because of all the contrasts; the smooth texture of the avocado and the crunchiness of the apples. It makes for a great summer meal.

2 boneless, skinless chicken breast halves
3/4 cup orange juice, divided
1 tbs. soy sauce
2 ripe avocados
2 Gala or Fuji apples
1/3 cup orange juice
1/2 cup vegetable oil
4 cups baby lettuces (mesclun)

Marinate chicken breasts in 1/2 cup of the orange juice mixed with soy sauce for 15 minutes. Prepare a hot grill, or preheat broiler. Peel and pit avocados; cut into 1-inch cubes. Quarter and core apples and cut into 1/2-inch cubes. Toss the avocados and apples with remaining 1/4 cup orange juice. Set aside.

Place chicken on grill or under broiler and cook until done, about 5 to 7 minutes per side. Brush with orange juice marinade once, and discard any remaining marinade. Cut cooked chicken into 1-inch cubes. Add to avocado-apple mixture. Pour oil over chicken, and very gently toss to mix. Place lettuce on a serving platter and top with chicken mixture.

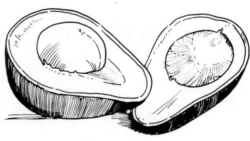

Time-Saver Tip: Wash, clean and slice radishes and bell peppers, and store them separately in plastic bags for quick salad additions.

SPICY ASIAN CHICKEN SALAD

Servings: 4

Try serving this bright salad with some purchased egg rolls for a complete meal.

1/4 cup vegetable oil
1/4 cup sesame oil
1/2 cup rice vinegar
1 tsp. crushed dried red peppers
2 tsp. soy sauce
2 tsp. sugar
9 cups shredded green and/or
  red cabbage (about 1 head)
4 carrots, shredded
8 green onions, slivered
3/4 cup peanuts
4 cups cooked chicken, shredded

In a small bowl, combine vegetable oil, sesame oil, rice vinegar, red peppers, soy sauce and sugar. Stir to mix and dissolve the sugar. Set aside.

In a large salad bowl, combine cabbage, carrots, onions, peanuts and chicken. Pour dressing over all and toss to mix. Let flavors blend for 10 minutes, toss again and serve.

Time-Saver Tip: Many grocery stores sell packages of shredded cabbage for cole slaw. Use enough to equal 9 cups (be sure to rinse before using).

PECAN CHICKEN SALAD

Servings: 4

Pecans and a light orange vinaigrette dress tender butter lettuce and chicken. My personal favorite is to prepare this with grilled or smoked chicken breasts.

1 tbs. butter
3/4 cup pecan halves
1/2 cup freshly squeezed orange juice
2 tbs. cider or rice vinegar
1/3 cup vegetable oil
1 tbs. honey
4 cooked chicken breast halves
12 cups torn butter lettuce

In a small skillet, heat butter over low heat. Add pecans and sauté until pecans are dark golden brown, about 5 minutes. Remove to paper towels to drain.

In a small bowl, combine orange juice, vinegar, oil and honey. Set aside. Cut chicken into 1/4-inch slices. Place chicken in a large salad bowl. Pour dressing over chicken and toss to coat. Let stand for 5 minutes. Add lettuce, toss again and serve.

MEXICAN SALAD

If you have any cooked chicken or shrimp, add it to this salad for a hearty meal.

¾ cup vegetable oil
½ cup vinegar
¾ tsp. salt
¾ cup chopped fresh cilantro
1 cup salsa
1½ cups chopped red onion
1 cup sliced olives

1½ cups cooked or canned black
   beans, rinsed and drained
1 cup sliced celery
12 cups torn romaine lettuce
1½ cups shredded cheddar cheese
1½ cups crushed tortilla chips

In a small bowl, mix together oil, vinegar, salt, cilantro and salsa. Set aside. In a large bowl, combine all remaining ingredients. Pour dressing over and toss well to mix. Serve immediately.

Time-Saver Tip: Cut up a head of lettuce, wash and spin dry. Store in an airtight container or locking plastic bag in the refrigerator for up to 5 days for salad on demand.

COLD BEEF SALAD

Servings: 4

I like to serve this using romaine lettuce, but it is also very good served on fresh baby spinach. The tangy dressing coats the beef with flavor.

1 lb. cooked, cold beef (such as leftover pot roast, or grilled steaks)
1 1/2 tsp. dried dill weed
3/4 tsp. dried thyme
1 1/4 cups vegetable oil
3 tbs. Dijon mustard
1/2 cup red wine vinegar
8 cups torn romaine lettuce
1/2 cup thinly sliced red onion

Slice beef into thin slices. Set aside.

In a small bowl, combine dill weed, thyme, oil, mustard and vinegar. Stir well to mix. Let stand for 15 minutes. In a medium bowl, pour dressing over beef and toss to evenly coat beef. To serve, place lettuce in a serving bowl and top with beef and dressing. Pour all dressing on beef. Scatter red onions over top and toss well prior to serving.

SHAVED VEGETABLE AND CRAB SALAD

Servings: 4

This is easiest to make with a food processor and a slicing blade. But you can do the same job by hand; just take time to slice the vegetables as thinly as possible.

1 cucumber, prefer European
10 radishes
1 carrot, peeled
½ cup thinly sliced red onion
1 lb. cooked crabmeat
½ cup rice vinegar
¼ cup vegetable oil
½ tsp. salt
¼ tsp. ground white pepper
1 tsp. sesame oil, optional

Using the slicing blade of a food processor, thinly slice cucumber, radishes and carrot. In a large bowl, combine cucumber, radishes, carrot, onion and crabmeat. In a small bowl, mix together vinegar, oil, salt, pepper and sesame oil, if using. Pour dressing over crab vegetable mixture and toss to coat. Serve immediately.

WARM SCALLOP AND SPINACH SALAD

Servings: 3-4

Tender white bay scallops and red bell peppers top deep green baby spinach for a dramatic salad.

1/4 cup fresh lemon juice
1 tbs. Dijon mustard
1/2 cup olive oil
1 lb. sea scallops
2 tbs. butter
4 cups baby spinach leaves
1/2 red bell pepper, thinly sliced

In a small bowl, stir together lemon juice, mustard and olive oil. Set aside.

Wash scallops and pat dry. Heat butter in a medium skillet over medium heat. Add scallops and cook just until opaque, about 2 minutes per side.

Place spinach on a serving platter. Sprinkle red bell pepper slices over spinach. Place hot scallops on top of red peppers. Drizzle lemon mustard dressing over scallops and serve immediately.

ORZO PASTA SALAD

Orzo is tiny rice-shaped pasta. It cooks quickly, and also cools down quickly in cold water, so you can have a hearty salad in less than 30 minutes.

$\frac{1}{2}$ lb. orzo pasta
$\frac{1}{2}$ cup minced red onion
1 large tomato, chopped
$\frac{1}{4}$ cup finely chopped green pepper
$\frac{1}{4}$ cup olive oil
$\frac{1}{4}$ balsamic vinegar
3 tbs. finely chopped fresh basil
$\frac{1}{2}$ tsp. salt
$\frac{1}{4}$ tsp. black pepper

Cook orzo according to package directions. When cooked, drain and rinse with cold water until cooled, and drain again. In a medium bowl, combine all ingredients, including cooled pasta, and toss to mix well. Serve chilled or at room temperature.

Time-Saver Tip: Bake or barbecue an extra chicken breast on the weekend for an easy addition to pasta or salads later that week.

FISH ENTRÉES

CAJUN PRAWNS

Saffron rice and bright green vegetables are perfect with these spicy prawns.

1/2 cup olive oil
1 tsp. cayenne pepper
2 cloves garlic, minced and pressed
1 tsp. Old Bay Seasoning
1 tbs. Worcestershire sauce
2 green onions, slivered
2 lb. medium prawns, peeled and cleaned

In a medium bowl, combine all ingredients. Marinate for 15 minutes at room temperature, stirring occasionally.

Heat oven broiler. Remove prawns from marinade, reserving any remaining marinade, and place on a broiler pan or in a shallow baking pan. Broil 4 to 6 inches from heat for about 6 minutes, turning occasionally, until prawns are just barely opaque in the center when tested with a fork. While prawns are cooking, bring remaining marinade to a boil and cook for 3 minutes. Keep warm. Place cooked prawns on a serving platter and drizzle with cooked marinade. Serve immediately.

LIME AND GARLIC PRAWNS

Servings: 4

These can be your entrée, or serve over greens as a main course salad. Either way, they are wonderful.

1/4 cup olive oil
1/4 cup fresh lime juice
4 cloves garlic, minced and pressed
1/4 tsp. salt
1 1/2 lb. large prawns, peeled and cleaned

Preheat broiler. In a small saucepan, combine olive oil, lime juice, garlic and salt. Heat just until warm and fragrant. Remove from heat. Dip each prawn into oil-lime mixture, and then arrange on a broiling pan or cookie sheet. Place under hot broiler for about 3 minutes, turning once. Prawns should be pink; do not overcook or they will be tough.

SHRIMP CURRY

Servings: 4

The combination of curry and cream coats the shrimp with a delicate sauce. Serve with sliced almonds on the side as a garnish, if desired.

2 tbs. butter or margarine
1/2 cup minced yellow onion
1/4 cup chicken broth
1/2 cup half-and-half
1 1/2 tsp. curry powder
1/2 tsp. salt
1 lb. cooked shrimp

In a medium saucepan, melt butter or margarine over medium heat. Add onion and sauté until onion begins to brown, about 8 to 10 minutes.

Add broth, half-and-half, curry powder and salt. Bring mixture just to a boil and reduce heat to medium-low. Stir frequently while sauce reduces, cooking for about 10 minutes. Add shrimp to sauce and stir to mix thoroughly. Continue to cook only until shrimp is heated, about 1 minute.

SHRIMP RISOTTO

Bay shrimp and herbs add a fresh taste and texture to a traditional Italian "comfort food."

1/4 cup butter
2 yellow onions, minced
2 cups Arborio rice
4 cups chicken broth
4 cups vegetable broth
2 cups cooked bay shrimp
1 tsp. dill weed
1/2 cup grated Parmesan cheese

In a large pot, melt butter over medium heat. Add onion and rice. Sauté until onion is translucent, about 5 minutes. Add broths. Increase heat to high and bring mixture to a boil. Reduce heat to low and simmer for 25 minutes, stirring constantly. Add shrimp and dill and stir well to mix. Remove from heat and stir in Parmesan cheese. Cover and let stand for 5 minutes before serving.

FETTUCINE WITH CRAB
AND TOMATO CREAM SAUCE

Servings: 4-6

This is one of my favorite ways to serve pasta. It's wonderful to serve to guests, as it is quick to prepare, and elegant.

8 oz. fettuccine
1 cup half-and-half
2 cups crabmeat
1 tsp. salt
2 cups coarsely chopped fresh tomatoes
2 tbs. slivered green onions
1/2 cup shredded Parmesan cheese

Begin cooking pasta according to package directions. While water heats and pasta cooks, prepare sauce.

In a medium saucepan, heat half-and-half over medium heat until very warm. Do not boil. Add crabmeat and salt, cover and keep warm.

Place cooked pasta in a serving bowl. Place chopped tomatoes and green onions on top of pasta. Pour warm cream and crab mixture over all. Toss to mix and sprinkle with Parmesan cheese. Serve immediately.

SCALLOPS WITH
SUN-DRIED TOMATO CREAM SAUCE

Tender scallops blanketed in a rosy pink sauce make a meal that your guests will compliment. The fact that it can be prepared in less than 20 minutes allows you to be with your guests, and not tied up in the kitchen. If using sun-dried tomatoes that are packed in oil, rinse the oil off before using. If they are dry-packed, they will rehydrate in the broth.

¾ cup sun-dried tomatoes	1½ cups cream
¾ tsp. salt	30 sea scallops (about 1½ lb.)
1½ cups chicken broth	⅓ cup butter
1 cup dry sherry	

Snip tomatoes into thin strips. In a medium saucepan, combine tomatoes, salt, chicken broth, sherry and cream. Bring mixture to a boil over high heat, stirring occasionally, until reduced, about 8 minutes. While sauce cooks, prepare scallops.

Rinse scallops in water and pat dry. Melt butter in a large skillet over medium heat. Add scallops and cook just until scallops are opaque in the center, about 2 minutes. Add sauce to scallops, stir and serve.

SESAME FISH

The flavorful sauce cooks while you broil or grill the fish pieces — the thick sauce is drizzled over the grilled fish and garnished with sesame seeds.

1 cup white wine
3 tbs. soy sauce
1-inch piece fresh ginger, peeled and sliced
2 cloves garlic, minced
1 tbs. sesame oil
4 fish fillets, such as orange roughy or sea bass, 4 oz. each
1 tsp. sesame seeds

Preheat broiler or prepare a hot grill.

In a medium saucepan, combine wine, soy sauce, ginger, garlic and 1 tsp. of the sesame oil. Bring mixture to a boil, reduce heat to low and simmer uncovered for 15 minutes to reduce.

While sauce is cooking, rub remaining sesame oil over all sides of fish fillets. Place fish under broiler or on grill and cook for about 8 to 10 minutes, or until opaque. Remove fish from heat and place on a serving platter. Pour sauce over fish and sprinkle with sesame seeds. Serve immediately.

GINGER GRILLED SALMON

This can also be prepared under a broiler, if you prefer.

4-inch piece fresh ginger, peeled and minced
$\frac{1}{2}$ cup sherry
1 tbs. soy sauce
$\frac{1}{4}$ cup honey
4 salmon steaks or 4 boneless, skinless fillets, about 6 oz. each

Combine ginger, sherry, soy sauce and honey in a shallow dish. Add salmon and marinate for 20 minutes, turning once.

Prepare a medium-hot grill. Place salmon on grill and cook for about 5 minutes on each side, basting with remaining marinade. After basting, discard any remaining marinade. Serve immediately.

HERBED RED SNAPPER PACKETS

These individual packets not only reduce cooking time, but also keep the fish moist and tender.

4 red snapper fillets, about 6 oz. each
1/2 tsp. dried rosemary
1 tsp. dried dill
1/4 tsp. salt

1/2 tsp. dried thyme
2 large fresh tomatoes, thinly sliced
3 tbs. butter, melted

Heat oven to 375°. Cut 4 pieces of aluminum foil, about 8 x 12 inches, or to fit the pieces of fish. Place a fillet on each piece of foil.

In a small bowl, combine rosemary, dill, salt and thyme. Stir to mix. Sprinkle an equal amount of herbs onto each fillet. Place an equal amount of tomato slices over herbs, overlapping if necessary to just cover fillets. Pour 2 tsp. melted butter over tomatoes on each fillet.

Fold foil over fillets, wrapping edges tightly. Place packets on a cookie sheet and bake for 12 minutes. Serve immediately.

Time Saver Tip: Assemble the packets earlier (up to 10 hours before serving), and just pop them into the oven when you are ready to serve.

POULTRY ENTRÉES

CHICKEN WITH PEPPER CREAM

Peppercorn melanges (a mixture of black, green, white and pink peppercorns) are available in most supermarkets in the spice section. For this recipe, do not grind the peppercorns, only crush them with a mallet.

2 tbs. butter
4 boneless chicken breast halves
1/2 tsp. peppercorn melange, crushed
1/2 cup sherry
3/4 cup half-and-half
1/2 tsp. salt

Heat butter in a large skillet over medium heat. Add chicken breasts and sauté until browned, about 10 minutes per side.

Add peppercorns, sherry, half-and-half and salt to skillet. Stir well to mix. Bring mixture to a boil and reduce heat to medium, allowing mixture to boil, uncovered, for about 5 minutes. Remove chicken to a serving platter and pour sauce over. Serve immediately.

CHICKEN AND SPINACH ENCHILADAS

If you don't have cooked chicken on hand, you can also use ground turkey or chicken — just brown about 1½ pounds of ground chicken or turkey, and use as you would the cooked chicken.

1 can (11 oz.) red or green enchilada sauce
2 cups shredded cooked chicken
1 pkg. (10 oz.) frozen chopped spinach, defrosted and squeezed dry
1 cup salsa
¾ cup shredded Monterey Jack cheese
8 flour or corn tortillas
½ cup sour cream

Heat oven to 450°. Pour ½ cup of the enchilada sauce onto the bottom of a 9-x-13-inch baking dish. Set aside.

In a medium bowl, combine chicken, spinach, salsa, and ½ cup of the cheese. Place about ½ cup of the chicken-spinach mixture on each tortilla and roll. Place in baking dish. Top with remaining enchilada sauce and sprinkle remaining cheese on top. Cover tightly with foil.

Bake until heated through, about 20 minutes. Remove from oven and transfer to a serving platter. Top with sour cream.

Time-Saver Tip: Warm up commercially prepared salsa to spoon on top of plain grilled meats, poultry or seafood.

ASIAN BLACK BEAN WINGS

You don't need to deep-fry wings — just a bit of shortening in a skillet will do. Black bean sauce is available in the Asian food section of most supermarkets. Many markets offer black bean sauces to which other flavorings are added, such as garlic or hot and spicy. Serve these on top of lightly steamed broccoli or sliced green or red bell peppers for an impressive presentation for guests.

2 cups shortening
1 1/2 lb. chicken wings, disjointed and tips discarded if you wish
1/2 cup all-purpose flour
1/2 tsp. garlic salt (or seasoning salt)
1/2 cup Asian black bean sauce
2 tbs. butter, melted

In a deep skillet, melt shortening over medium-high heat. Place chicken wings, flour and salt in a large plastic bag and shake to coat. Remove chicken from bag, shake to remove excess flour and set aside. Heat oven to 300° to keep cooked wings warm.

When shortening reaches 375°, place only enough wings in skillet for a single layer, and do not crowd. Fry until golden brown, about 5 to 7 minutes per side, and turn. As wings cook, remove them to a paper towel and keep warm. Continue adding wings to skillet as you remove cooked ones.

While you are cooking wings, heat black bean sauce and butter together over low heat until hot, and keep warm until all wings have been cooked. When all wings have been cooked, place wings and black bean sauce-butter mixture in a large bowl. Toss until evenly coated and serve immediately.

Time-Saver Tip: Add 1 cup crushed drained pineapple to 1 cup teriyaki sauce for a fresh take on regular teriyaki chicken or beef.

CHICKEN IN RED WINE

True coq au vin takes a lot of time to simmer. Here we have reduced the amount of time needed, because you start the wine reduction sauce at the same time you start cooking the chicken.

3 cups red wine
1 can (14½ oz) chicken broth
6 slices bacon
1 chicken, cut into pieces

1 yellow onion, chopped
1 lb. mushrooms, sliced
½ tsp. salt

In a medium saucepan, combine wine and broth. Bring mixture to a boil over high heat and reduce heat to medium-high, keeping a rolling boil at all times.

As wine mixture boils, brown bacon in a Dutch oven or large stew pot over high heat until crisp. Remove bacon and drain off all but 2 tbs. bacon fat from pot. Return pot to heat and add chicken. Brown chicken on all sides, about 10 minutes. While chicken is browning, crumble bacon into boiling wine mixture.

When chicken is brown, add onion, mushrooms and salt to pot. Stir to mix. Pour hot wine mixture over chicken and bring to a full boil. Reduce heat to medium and simmer, uncovered, for 15 minutes, or until chicken is cooked through, stirring occasionally. Serve on a warm platter.

CHICKEN WITH APPLES

This is a great entrée to serve in the fall when apples are at their peak. Serve with buttered egg noodles to catch all the delicious sauce.

1 tbs. vegetable oil	1/2 cup chicken broth
6 chicken breast halves	1/4 tsp. dried thyme
2 tbs. all-purpose flour	1/2 tsp. salt
1 cup apple juice	3 Winesap or Gala apples

In a large deep skillet or Dutch oven, heat oil over medium-high heat. Add chicken and cook until browned, about 5 minutes on each side.

In a small bowl, dissolve flour in apple juice. Add apple juice, broth, thyme and salt to skillet, increase heat to high and bring mixture to a boil. Reduce heat to low, cover and simmer for 15 minutes.

While chicken simmers, core apples and cut into thin slices. When chicken is done, remove breasts from sauce, arrange on a serving platter and keep warm. Add apple slices to sauce and increase heat to high. Cook uncovered until apples are just tender, about 5 minutes. Spoon apples and sauce over chicken. Serve immediately.

CHICKEN WITH ITALIAN SAUSAGE AND PEPPERS

Try this on top of warm ready-to-serve polenta for a traditional Italian meal.

4 Italian sausages, hot or mild
1 whole chicken, cut into pieces
2 cloves garlic, minced
2 green bell peppers, cored and thinly sliced

1 can (16 oz.) whole tomatoes
1 yellow onion, thinly sliced
$1/2$ tsp. salt
$1/2$ tsp. basil
$1/2$ tsp. oregano

Heat a large pot or Dutch oven over medium-high heat. Add sausages and cook until lightly browned on all sides, about 5 to 10 minutes. Remove from pot and let cool slightly. Add chicken to pot and brown on all sides, about 10 minutes. While chicken is cooking, cut cooked sausage into $1/2$-inch-thick slices; set aside.

When chicken is browned, add all remaining ingredients at once, including sliced sausages. Increase heat to high and bring to a boil. Cover, reduce heat to medium-low and simmer for 10 to 15 minutes, or until chicken and sausages are cooked through. Serve immediately.

Time-Saver Tip: Prepare your vegetables as the sausages and chicken cook, instead of before you begin cooking.

LEMON CHICKEN

This has all the flavors of the lemon chicken found in Chinese restaurants, but it's quicker to prepare, and has less fat than the restaurant's deep-fried version.

4 boneless, skinless chicken breasts
1 tbs. vegetable oil
2/3 cup freshly squeezed lemon juice
3 tbs. sugar

1 1/3 cups water
4 tsp. cornstarch
1 tsp. catsup
1/2 lb. snow pea pods

Place chicken between 2 pieces of plastic wrap or waxed paper and pound until 1/4-inch thick. Slice chicken into 1-inch-wide strips.

In a medium bowl, combine lemon juice, sugar, water, cornstarch and catsup. Stir until smooth and set aside.

Heat a large skillet over medium-high heat. Add oil and chicken. Sauté chicken until it begins to brown on all sides, about 10 minutes. Add sauce mixture, stirring constantly, and increase heat to high. When sauce begins to boil, reduce heat to low and simmer for 5 minutes to thicken sauce. Add pea pods and stir to mix. Continue to cook on low until pea pods are tender-crisp, about 3 to 5 minutes. Serve immediately.

PACIFIC RIM CHICKEN

Servings: 4

Pounding chicken breasts helps to keep the chicken tender when cooking quickly. It also allows seasoning to penetrate the meat easier.

4 boneless skinless chicken breast halves
1 tsp. ground ginger
1 tbs. vegetable oil
1 can (20 oz.) pineapple tidbits or chunks, juice reserved
2 tbs. brown sugar
1 tbs. cornstarch
1/4 cup sliced green onions

Place chicken breast halves between 2 pieces of plastic wrap. Pound breasts to uniform thickness. Cut each breast into 2 equal pieces. Combine ginger and oil in a small bowl. Rub ginger-oil mixture into chicken.

Heat a skillet over medium-high heat. Add chicken (in two batches if necessary) and cook until golden, about 7 minutes per side; remove from skillet and keep warm.

Add pineapple and juice, brown sugar and cornstarch to skillet. Bring mixture to a boil, stirring constantly. Reduce heat to low and return chicken to skillet. Cover and simmer for 10 minutes. Just before serving, sprinkle with sliced green onions.

RED-SAUCED CHICKEN

There are many uses for canned enchilada sauce other than just for enchiladas. Here it is used as the base of a spicy, saucy chicken; try this in fresh flour tortillas, or served over hot white rice.

4 boneless, skinless chicken breast halves
2 tbs. vegetable oil
2 cloves garlic, minced
1 can (14 oz.) red enchilada sauce
1/2 tsp. salt
flour tortillas or hot white rice, optional

Place chicken breast between 2 pieces of plastic wrap, and using a kitchen mallet, pound to 1/4- to 1/2-inch thickness. Slice chicken into 1-inch strips. Place chicken, oil and garlic in a medium bowl and toss to coat. Marinate for 10 minutes.

Heat a large skillet over medium-high heat. Add chicken mixture and sauté until chicken begins to brown, about 10 minutes. Add enchilada sauce and salt and bring mixture to a boil. Reduce heat to low and simmer for 5 minutes. Serve with flour tortillas or over hot white rice.

CHICKEN VERDE

This chicken dish is based on chile verde — have lots of bread on hand to get all the delicious juices.

2 tbs. vegetable oil
1 chicken, cut into pieces
2 cans (14½ oz. each) chicken broth
3 cans (4 oz. each) chopped green chiles
½ tsp. ground cumin
1 yellow onion, chopped
3 cloves garlic, minced

In a large skillet, heat oil over medium-high heat. Add chicken and brown on all sides, about 15 minutes.

While chicken is browning, combine broth, chiles and cumin in a medium saucepan. Bring to a boil over high heat, reduce to medium and continue to boil to reduce sauce.

When chicken is browning, add onion and garlic. Continue to cook until onion is translucent. Pour hot sauce over chicken and continue to cook until chicken is done, about 10 more minutes.

SICILIAN-STYLE STUFFED CHICKEN BREASTS

Servings: 4

A small amount of flavorful stuffing is all you need to enhance boneless, skinless chicken breasts.

1/4 cup snipped dry-packed sun-dried
   tomatoes
2 tbs. boiling water
4 boneless skinless chicken breast halves

1/4 cup coarsely chopped pitted
   kalamata olives
2 tbs. pine nuts
1/4 cup butter, melted, divided

Heat oven to 375°. Prepare a baking sheet by spraying with nonstick spray.

Place sun-dried tomatoes in a small bowl. Pour boiling water over tomatoes, stir and let stand for 5 minutes. Place chicken breast halves between two sheets of waxed paper or plastic wrap. Pound breasts to about 3/8-inch thick.

In a medium bowl, combine tomatoes and any remaining water, olives and pine nuts. Place about 2 tablespoons of the mixture down the center of each piece of chicken. Fold sides of chicken over tomato mixture to enclose, and lay chicken seam-side down on baking sheet. Brush tops of chicken rolls with about 1 tsp. of the melted butter. Bake for 20 minutes, or until chicken is lightly browned and feels firm when pressed. Remove from oven and cut into 1-inch-thick slices. Drizzle remaining melted butter over slices and serve.

COUNTRY FRENCH CHICKEN

This entrée is a meal in one skillet. Serve with a simple salad and some crusty bread, and your dinner is complete.

1 tbs. vegetable oil
4 chicken breast halves or 8 thighs
1 cup chicken broth
1/4 cup grained mustard

1/4 cup sherry
1 tsp. salt
4 medium-sized red-skinned potatoes
1 lb. fresh green beans

Heat a large skillet or Dutch oven over medium heat. Add oil and swirl to coat bottom of pan. Add chicken and cook until lightly browned, about 8 minutes per side.

In a small bowl, combine broth, mustard, sherry and salt. Stir to mix, and set aside.

Slice potatoes into 1/2-thick slices (do not peel). Trim ends off green beans. Add potatoes, green beans and chicken broth mixture to browned chicken pieces. Increase heat to high and bring mixture to a boil. Reduce heat to medium-low, cover and simmer for 10 minutes, or until potatoes are tender. Serve immediately.

Time-Saver Tip: Grill halved, cored fruits such as peaches, nectarines or pears at the same time you grill chicken.

RED CURRY

A variation of standard curry, this is more of a stew. Try serving with lots of hot steamed rice.

4 boneless, skinless chicken breast halves
2 tbs. vegetable oil
1 cup chopped yellow onion
1 cup chopped green bell pepper
2 cans (14½ oz. each) ready-cut tomatoes
2 tsp. curry powder
1 tsp. salt
1 tsp. garlic powder

Cut chicken breasts into 2-inch chunks. Heat oil in a medium skillet over medium-high heat. Add chicken and sauté until chicken is opaque and is just beginning to brown, about 10 minutes. Reduce heat to medium-low.

Add onion, bell pepper, tomatoes, curry powder, salt and garlic powder. Stir to mix and simmer for 15 minutes. Serve hot.

ORANGE-GLAZED GAME HENS

Servings: 4

Try serving this with Rice with Almonds, *page 94. They make an attractive presentation together.*

2 Cornish game hens, split into halves
2 tbs. butter, melted
½ cup frozen orange juice concentrate, thawed
½ cup chicken broth
¼ cup sherry

Heat oven to 475°. Place game hen halves in a 9-x-13-inch baking dish, skin-side up. Rub skin with butter and bake until light-golden, about 20 minutes. While hens bake, make sauce.

In a small saucepan, combine orange juice concentrate, chicken broth and sherry. Bring mixture to a boil, and reduce heat to medium. Cook sauce for about 5 minutes, or until a bit thickened. Keep warm.

When hens are done, pour glaze over them. Return to oven and bake for an additional 5 minutes. Serve hens with sauce.

TURKEY IN WHITE WINE HERB SAUCE

Servings: 4-6

Most stores carry turkey cutlets, but if they don't, just use a fresh turkey breast (about 1 1/2-2 lb.) and slice into 1/4-inch-thick slices.

1 cup flour
1 1/2 lb. turkey cutlets
1/4 cup butter
1/4 cup olive oil
1/2 cup white wine
1/2 cup heavy cream

In a shallow plate, combine flour, tarragon, thyme and salt. Dredge cutlets in flour mixture and set aside.

In a large skillet, melt butter and olive oil together over medium-high heat. Add cutlets and sauté until golden, about 3 to 4 minutes per side. Transfer to a plate and keep warm. Add white wine and cream to pan and bring mixture to a boil, scraping up any bits from the bottom of skillet. Boil until slightly thickened, about 4 minutes. Pour sauce over cooked cutlets and serve.

MEAT ENTRÉES

GARLICKY STEAKS

This may seem like a lot of garlic, but it helps form a nice crust on the beef, and it becomes sweet and mellow when cooked.

8 cloves garlic
4 tsp. olive oil
1/2 tsp. salt
4 sirloin steaks, 1-inch thick

Place garlic, olive oil and salt in a blender container. Pulse on high until you have a paste. Pat paste onto both sides of each steak, being sure to use all paste. Set aside for 10 minutes. Preheat a broiler or prepare a hot grill.

Place meat about 5 to 6 inches away from heat source. Cook for about 4 to 5 minutes per side for medium-rare. Turn steaks over only once.

Time-Saver Tip: Mix up a red wine marinade for steaks and place 1/4 cup marinade with each 4-ounce piece of meat into locking freezer bags. Remove from the freezer in the morning, and you'll have nicely marinated steaks that evening.

FAJITA-STYLE STIR-FRY

This recipe has the flavors of Mexican fajitas cooked in the Asian style with a wok. Serve with hot rice or with flour tortillas.

1 lb. beef
1/4 tsp. cayenne pepper
1 tsp. ground cumin
2 tsp. vegetable oil, divided
1 red bell pepper, stem and seeds
   removed, thinly sliced

1 green bell pepper, stem and seeds
   removed, thinly sliced
1 yellow onion, thinly sliced
1/2 tsp. salt
1 lime

Cut beef into thin (1/8-inch-thick) strips. In a small bowl, combine meat, cayenne pepper and cumin. Stir to coat beef strips evenly.

Heat a wok or large skillet over medium-high heat. Add 1 tsp. oil and swirl to coat bottom of pan. Add beef and stir frequently until browned, about 4 minutes. Transfer beef to a platter and keep warm while you prepare vegetables.

Pour remaining oil into wok. Add peppers, onion and salt to oil. Stir-fry until peppers are tender-crisp, about 2 to 4 minutes. Add beef to wok and stir to heat through.

Place beef and vegetables on a serving plate and squeeze lime juice over all. Serve immediately.

GRILLED RIB-EYE STEAKS

Tender beef rib-eye steaks are sandwiched between grilled strips of zucchini and artichokes. It is a simple recipe to prepare, but dramatic in taste and presentation.

2 boneless beef rib-eye steaks, about 1-inch thick, 12 oz. each
2 jars (4 oz. each) marinated artichoke hearts or bottoms
2 large green zucchini

Prepare a hot grill. While grill heats, trim steaks of any excess fat. Drain artichokes, reserving marinade in a shallow dish. Add steaks to marinade, turning once to coat. Marinate for 5 minutes on each side.

Trim ends off zucchini. Cut into ½-inch-thick strips lengthwise, about 3 or 4 slices for each zucchini. Brush zucchini slices with some of the artichoke marinade.

Place steaks on grill about 4 to 6 inches from heat. Grill for 5 to 7 minutes on each side for rare, 7 to 9 minutes for medium, or 9 to 11 minutes for well done. Place zucchini and artichokes on grill for about 3 minutes on each side, or until zucchini is lightly cooked, but not soft. Brush steaks and vegetables often with marinade as they cook. Discard any used marinade.

To serve, place zucchini strips on a plate. Place steaks over zucchini and top with artichokes. Serve immediately.

HERB GARLIC-GRILLED LAMB

Servings: 4

Quickly marinating the lamb gives the meat flavor, and helps create a beautiful herbed crust.

4 cloves garlic, minced
2 tbs. minced fresh rosemary
2 tbs. minced fresh sage
$\frac{1}{2}$ cup olive oil
2 tbs. cider vinegar
4 loin lamb chops, about 1$\frac{1}{2}$ inches thick

In a shallow dish, combine garlic, rosemary, sage, olive oil and vinegar. Stir to mix well. Add lamb and turn chops over once to coat. Marinate for 15 minutes at room temperature, turning once.

Heat a grill to medium-high heat. Remove chops from marinade and place on grill, keeping as much herb mixture on meat as possible. Discard any remaining marinade. Cook for 4 to 5 minutes on each side, turning once. Serve immediately.

LAMB CURRY IN PITAS

Instead of using cubes of lamb, we have used ground lamb instead. This not only cooks quicker, but is easier to eat in pita breads. The cucumber salad is a cool contrast to the spicy meat mixture.

1 lb. ground lamb
1 yellow onion, minced
3 tbs. curry powder
$1/4$ cup water
$1/2$ tsp. salt
2 tbs. tomato paste

1 medium cucumber, peeled and
  sliced
2 green onions, thinly sliced
1 cup plain yogurt
8 whole pita breads, cut in half

In a medium skillet, brown lamb over medium-high heat. Drain any excess fat. Add onion, curry powder, water, salt and tomato paste. Stir to mix. Reduce heat to low, cover and simmer for 15 minutes. Prepare cucumber salad while meat simmers.

In a medium bowl, combine cucumber, green onions and yogurt. Stir to mix, and set aside.

To serve, gently separate pitas. Fill partially with some of the meat mixture and top with cucumber salad.

LEMON LAMB CHOPS

Servings: 4

A fast marinade and frequent basting gives simple lamb chops a fresh new taste.

1/4 cup fresh lemon juice
grated zest of 1 lemon
1/3 cup olive oil
2 tbs. minced fresh parsley
1/4 tsp. salt
1/4 tsp. freshly ground black pepper
4 lamb chops, about 3/4-inch thick

In a shallow bowl, mix together lemon juice, grated zest, oil, parsley, salt and pepper. Add lamb chops to marinade, turning once to coat. Marinate for 15 minutes, turning every 5 minutes. Preheat broiler.

Remove chops from marinade and place on a broiling rack. Place under hot broiler and cook until nicely browned on both sides, about 4 to 5 minutes per side for medium. Baste frequently with marinade. Serve immediately.

MEXICAN PORK SKEWERS

Serve with slices of fresh avocado for a different summer barbecue.

1 lb. tiny new red potatoes
4 boneless pork chops, 1-inch thick
2 tbs. vegetable oil
1 1/2 tsp. ground cumin
1/2 tsp. cayenne pepper
4 cloves garlic, minced or pressed
1/2 tsp. salt

Prepare a medium-hot barbecue grill. Place potatoes in a medium saucepan and cover with water. Bring to a boil over high heat, reduce heat to medium and cook until potatoes are just tender, about 15 minutes. While potatoes cook, prepare pork.

Trim all visible fat from pork. Cut into 1-inch cubes and place into a shallow bowl. Add all other ingredients, except potatoes, and toss to coat evenly. Marinate for 15 minutes. Drain potatoes when done and rinse in cold water until cool. Add to pork and toss to coat with marinade. Skewer two or three pieces of pork, followed by a potato, and add more pork. Alternate as desired to fill 8 skewers.

Grill skewers for about 5 minutes each side. Remove from grill and serve.

PLUM-SAUCED RIBS

Par-boiling the ribs helps remove the excess fat and speeds up cooking time. You can find plum sauce in most grocery stores in the Asian foods section.

2 qt. water
1/4 cup soy sauce
2 lb. pork ribs
3/4 cup plum sauce
1/3 cup sherry

Heat oven to 450°. Combine water and soy sauce in a large pot and bring to a boil over high heat.

Cut rack of ribs into individual ribs. Cut boneless meat into 2-inch pieces. When water boils, add ribs and meat. Allow water to return to a boil and boil on high for 3 minutes. Remove ribs and drain off all water and fat.

While ribs are boiling, mix together plum sauce and sherry. Place boiled ribs in a 9-x-13-inch baking dish and pour plum sauce over ribs. Stir to coat all meat evenly. Bake for 15 minutes. Serve with thickened sauce from baking dish.

PORK LOIN WITH PEACHES

You can use either fresh or canned peaches for this dish, so you can prepare it any time of year.

1 tbs. butter
1½ lb. pork tenderloin
4 large ripe peaches, or 8 canned
　peach halves

8 tsp. bourbon or whisky
1 tsp. ground ginger

Heat oven to 400°. In a large skillet, melt butter over medium-high heat. Add pork loin and brown well on all sides. Transfer to a baking sheet and bake for about 15 minutes, or until an instant-read meat thermometer reads 160° when inserted in the thickest part. While pork bakes, prepare peaches.

If using fresh peaches, peel and cut in half, discarding pit. Using a fork, pierce the cut side about ¼-inch deep many times (do not pierce all the way through). Pour 1 teaspoon bourbon over each cut peach. Sprinkle ⅛ tsp. ginger over peaches. Place peaches cut-side up on a baking sheet. Set aside until pork has finished baking.

When pork is done, remove from oven and set aside for 10 minutes. Heat broiler and broil peaches until very hot, about 7 to 10 minutes. Slice pork against the grain and place on a serving platter. Arrange peaches around meat and serve.

PORK MEDALLIONS WITH CRANBERRIES

Servings: 4

This treatment for tender pork slices makes a great fall entrée, when fresh cranberries are available.

1 lb. pork tenderloin
salt
2 tbs. butter
$1/2$ cup fresh cranberries
$1/4$ cup white wine
$1/3$ cup brown sugar

Slice pork into $1/2$-inch-thick slices. Sprinkle each piece lightly with salt. In a large skillet, melt butter over medium heat. Add pork and cook for 3 minutes per side. Remove pork from skillet and arrange on a serving platter; keep warm while you prepare sauce. Add cranberries, wine and sugar to skillet and stir to mix. Reduce heat to low, cover and simmer for 10 minutes. Taste sauce and, if desired, add a bit more brown sugar. Pour sauce over pork medallions and serve.

PORK WITH HOISIN SAUCE

Servings: 4

Hoisin sauce glazes these pork chops and creates a rich, sweet sauce.

2 tbs. butter
4 pork chops
1/2 cup hoisin sauce
2 tbs. honey
1/4 cup white wine
2 tbs. slivered green onion

In a medium skillet, melt butter over medium heat. Add chops and brown, about 10 minutes per side. Add hoisin, honey and wine, and stir to mix. Turn chops over to coat in sauce. Cover and reduce heat to low. Simmer for 10 minutes and serve immediately.

Time-Saver Tip: Double up a batch of your favorite meat loaf recipe, and freeze one for a future dinner. If you make each recipe into two or three small loaves, rather than one, they will bake faster.

RUSTIC MEAT AND VEGETABLE PASTA

Servings: 4-6

This rich meat-sauced pasta is an Italian classic.

4 oz. lean ground beef
4 oz. Italian sausage
1/2 cup chopped carrots
1 yellow onion, minced
4 oz. white mushrooms, chopped
1 clove garlic, minced

1/2 tsp. dried oregano
1 can (28 oz.) Italian plum tomatoes,
  coarsely chopped
1/2 tsp. salt
1 1/2 lb. dried ziti, rigatoni or fusilli pasta

In a large saucepan, combine ground beef and Italian sausage (if using sausage in casings, remove sausage, crumble into ground beef and discard casings). Brown meat over high heat, stirring frequently to crumble meat. Drain off all fat.

Add carrots, onions, mushrooms and garlic. Stir to mix into meat. Reduce heat to medium and continue to cook until onion is translucent. Add oregano, tomatoes and salt, and increase heat to medium-high. Bring sauce to a boil, cover and reduce heat to simmer. Simmer for 15 minutes; while sauce is simmering, cook pasta according to package directions. Drain pasta and serve with hot sauce.

STEAKS WITH GREEN PEPPERCORN SAUCE

Servings: 4

This is a classic sauce to serve with your favorite cut of meat, and it is impressive enough to serve to guests.

4 medium beef steaks
1/4 tsp. salt
1/4 tsp. black pepper
2 tbs. butter

1 tbs. all-purpose flour
2 cups beef broth
1/4 cup sherry
1 tbs. green peppercorns

Season steaks with salt and pepper. Set aside.

In a medium saucepan, melt butter over medium heat. Add flour and stir until smooth. Using a wire whisk, stir in beef broth and sherry, mixing well to prevent lumps from forming. Add peppercorns and increase heat to high. Bring mixture to a boil and reduce heat to medium. Cook uncovered until liquid is reduced to 1 cup, about 20 minutes.

While sauce is reducing, broil steaks to preferred doneness. Keep warm and serve with peppercorn sauce.

VELVET BEEF

This recipe is for stir-fried beef and mushrooms, but no sauce. The beef is tender and flavorful, and the vegetables add texture.

1 lb. beef, thinly sliced
2 tsp. soy sauce
2 tsp. sherry or white wine
4 tsp. cornstarch
1 tbs. vegetable oil
8 oz. mushrooms, sliced
1/2 cup sliced water chestnuts

In a small bowl, combine beef, soy sauce and sherry. Toss to mix and marinate for 5 minutes. Add cornstarch and mix thoroughly to coat all beef. Set aside for 5 minutes.

Heat oil in a wok or large skillet over high heat. Add beef and stir-fry until cooked through and beginning to brown, about 5 to 10 minutes. Remove beef from wok and keep warm. Add mushrooms and water chestnuts, and stir-fry until mushrooms release moisture and begin to brown, about 10 minutes. Add beef to wok and toss to mix. Serve immediately.

VEGETARIAN ENTRÉES

POLENTA WITH SUN-DRIED TOMATOES

Although polenta dishes are still in the "trendy" stage, it is old-fashioned comfort food for Italians. This is very filling as your entrée — try it with Sautéed Spinach and Pine Nuts, page 81, for a classic Italian supper.

5 cups chicken broth
1 cup polenta
1/3 cup minced sun-dried tomatoes
1/2 tsp. salt
2 tbs. minced chives
1/2 cup shredded Parmesan cheese

In a medium saucepan, heat chicken broth to boiling over high heat. Using a wire whisk and stirring constantly, sprinkle in polenta. Continue stirring and add salt and sun-dried tomatoes. Reduce heat to medium low, cover and cook for 25 minutes, stirring frequently. Remove from heat and stir in chives. Spoon into a serving bowl and sprinkle with Parmesan cheese. Serve immediately.

BAKED CHILE RELLENOS

Servings: 4-6

True chile rellenos take quite a while to prepare. This easy baked version tastes just like the original, but is much easier and quicker to the table.

8 eggs
1 cup milk
6 tbs. all-purpose flour
1 tsp. salt
2 cans (4 oz. each) whole green chiles
2½ cups shredded cheddar cheese, divided
salsa or picante sauce, optional

Heat oven to 425°. Spray a 9-x-13-inch baking dish with nonstick spray.

In a blender, combine eggs, milk, flour and salt. Pulse until thoroughly blended. Pour 1 cup of the mixture into the bottom of prepared baking dish.

Slice chiles along one side to create a pocket. Place ¼ cup shredded cheese in each chile. Place stuffed chiles in baking dish next to each other. Pour remaining egg mixture over stuffed chiles. Sprinkle with any remaining cheese.

Bake for 20 minutes. Remove from oven and serve immediately. Spoon salsa or picante sauce on top of each serving, if desired.

GRILLED RATATOUILLE

This dish is perfect for a summer evening, because everything is cooked out-side. Serve with lots of fresh French bread to help soak up all the juices.

1 small eggplant
1 red bell pepper
1 green bell pepper
2 zucchini
1 carrot, peeled
1 yellow onion
4 large beefsteak tomatoes
1/4 cup olive oil
2 cloves garlic, left whole
1/2 tsp. salt
1/4 tsp. black pepper

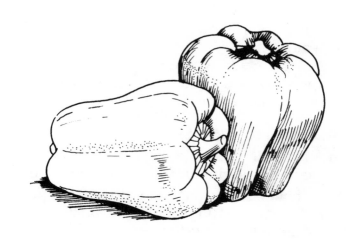

Prepare a hot grill. Cut eggplant lengthwise into 4 slices. Quarter and core bell peppers. Cut zucchini in half lengthwise. Cut carrot in half lengthwise. Peel onion and cut into thick rings, but do not separate. Cut tomatoes in half. Brush vegetables with olive oil, reserving any remaining oil.

Place all vegetables and garlic cloves on the grill. Cook until tender, about 5 minutes per side (peppers will take a bit less time, zucchini and carrots a bit more). When done, let vegetables cool until you can handle them and cut into bite-sized pieces. Smash garlic into remaining olive oil and add to vegetables. Add salt and pepper, taste and adjust seasonings. Serve immediately, or cool to room temperature.

Time-Saver Tip: Try a fresh herb omelet for dinner — serve it with fresh bread and a crisp salad.

CHEDDAR CHILE FONDUE

This is a Tex-Mex version of the classic dish. Serve with raw vegetables or other "dippers," and a giant pitcher of margaritas and bottles of cold beer.

¼ cup butter
2 tbs. flour
1 cup milk
4 cups shredded cheddar cheese
1 can (4 oz.) diced green chiles
1 cup tomato-based salsa, hot or mild

DIPPERS
jicama
celery
red or green bell pepper pieces
cauliflower or broccoli florets
Chinese pea pods
carrot slices or baby carrots
zucchini slices
French bread cubes
tortilla chips or corn chips

In a large saucepan, melt butter over medium heat. Sprinkle in flour and stir well. Using a wire whisk and the milk, and stir constantly until smooth. Continue to cook over medium heat until thickened, and just coming to a boil. Add cheese, chiles and salsa. Stir to mix, and continue to cook over medium heat until cheese is completely melted, about 10 minutes.

Transfer to a fondue pot, if desired, and keep warm over a heat source. Serve with raw vegetables, bread and tortilla chips.

Time-Saver Tip: Instead of using pizza sauce on a prebaked pizza crust, use pesto, barbecue sauce or any commercial pasta sauce. Alfredo or four-cheese sauce is terrific topped with shredded mozzarella; for a nonvegetarian entrée, add cooked bay shrimp.

PASTA WITH ARTICHOKE
AND TOMATO SAUCE

Servings: 4-6

If you have a garden and grow tomatoes, this sauce is a perfect use for those really ripe tomatoes. If you can't find really nice fresh tomatoes, use canned.

2 tbs. olive oil
2 cloves garlic, minced
1 yellow onion, minced
2 lb. fresh tomatoes, peeled and
    chopped

1 can (14 oz.) artichoke hearts, drained
    and coarsely chopped
1 tsp. dried rosemary
1 tsp. salt
1 lb. fettuccine
1 cup shredded Parmesan cheese

In a large stockpot, heat olive oil over medium heat. Add garlic and onion and sauté until vegetables begin to brown, about 5 minutes. Add tomatoes, artichoke heats, rosemary and salt. Bring mixture to a boil, stirring frequently. Reduce heat to low and simmer uncovered for 20 minutes to reduce. While sauce is simmering, cook pasta according to package directions.

Pour sauce over cooked pasta and toss to mix. Serve immediately and pass shredded cheese.

ANGEL HAIR PASTA
WITH SUN-DRIED TOMATOES

This light meal is also great to serve as a side dish for 8.

1 cup chicken broth
1/2 cup oil-packed sun-dried tomatoes,
   thinly sliced
8 oz. angel hair pasta
1/4 cup olive oil

3 cloves garlic, minced
1/2 tsp. salt
1/4 tsp. pepper
1/2 cup minced fresh basil
1/2 cup shredded Parmesan cheese

In a small saucepan, heat chicken broth to a boil. Remove from heat and add tomatoes. Stir, cover and set aside for 10 minutes. While it is setting, begin pasta.

Prepare pasta according to package directions; drain. Return pasta to cooking pot. Add oil and garlic, and toss to coat. Add broth and tomatoes, salt, pepper and basil, and toss to mix thoroughly.

Place pasta in a serving bowl and top with Parmesan. Serve immediately.

Time Saver Tip: You can cut sun-dried tomatoes into thin strips faster with scissors than with a knife!

FETTUCCINE WITH SPINACH AND TOMATOES

Servings: 4

The spinach is not cooked in this dish — the heat of the pasta wilts it just enough. It is also a pasta dish with a lot of sauce and vegetables in proportion to the actual pasta.

2 tbs. olive oil
2 cloves garlic, minced
1/2 cup pine nuts
1/4 cup chopped fresh basil
1 tsp. salt

1 1/2 lb. fresh Roma tomatoes, chopped
1 lb. fresh spinach, washed and
   stemmed
1/2 lb. fettuccine
1/2 cup shredded Parmesan cheese

In a medium saucepan, heat oil over medium heat. Add garlic and pine nuts, and sauté until nuts begin to turn golden. Add basil, salt and tomatoes; stir and reduce heat to low. Simmer for 5 minutes, or until heated through.

Prepare fettuccine according to package directions. Drain. Place cooked fettuccine in a serving bowl and place spinach on top. Pour tomato sauce over spinach and toss to mix. Set aside for 2 minutes, toss again and sprinkle with Parmesan cheese. Serve immediately.

VEGETABLES

ASPARAGUS WITH RED PEPPER BUTTER

Servings: 4

Sweet red bell peppers and butter form a simple sauce. The bright sauce and the green asparagus are a sure sign that spring has arrived.

1/4 cup butter
1/2 cup chopped red bell peppers
1/4 tsp. salt
2 lb. fresh asparagus
1 cup water

In a small saucepan, melt butter over medium heat. Add bell peppers and sauté until peppers are very soft, but not browned, about 5 to 8 minutes. Pour peppers and butter into a blender container and pulse until smooth. Keep warm while you prepare asparagus.

In a large shallow skillet, lay spears about 2 or 3 layers deep. Add 1 cup water and bring to a boil. Cover and reduce heat to medium. Cook to desired tenderness (tender-crisp will take about 4 minutes; fully tender will take about 7 minutes). Drain.

Place asparagus on a serving platter. Drizzle pepper sauce over spears and serve immediately.

BROWN MUSHROOMS AND PEARL ONIONS

Servings: 4-6

This hearty side dish works well with beef and pork dishes.

¾ lb. pearl onions or boiling onions
2 tbs. butter
1½ lb. brown mushrooms, halved
½ tsp. salt
2 tbs. chopped fresh parsley

In a medium saucepan, bring 1 quart of water to a boil. Add onions in their skins and boil until tender, about 10 minutes. Drain and rinse with cool water. Peel onions and trim tops and bottoms.

In a large skillet, melt butter over medium heat. Add mushrooms and salt and sauté until mushrooms begin to release moisture. Add onions and sauté for another 5 minutes, or until liquid has evaporated and mushrooms and onions are beginning to brown. Transfer to a serving bowl and sprinkle with parsley.

COLD SAUCED BEAN SPROUTS

These cold bean sprouts can be a light appetizer or a vegetable side dish.

about 2 qt. water
1 lb. fresh bean sprouts
2 tbs. vegetable oil
2 tsp. sesame oil
$\frac{1}{2}$ tsp. salt
2 tbs. rice vinegar
$\frac{1}{4}$ tsp. ground ginger

In a large pot, bring water to a boil. Plunge bean sprouts into water and boil for 2 minutes. Immediately drain and rinse in cold water to cool quickly; drain again.

In a large bowl, combine oils, salt, vinegar and ginger. Stir to mix. Add cooled, drained bean sprouts and toss to coat. Serve at room temperature or place in the refrigerator to chill.

CREAM-GLAZED CARROTS

Servings: 4-6

Baby carrots are very sweet when cooked, and most people serve them plain with a bit of butter. The simple cream glazing adds a sophisticated touch.

3 tbs. butter
4 cups baby carrots
1/4 cup apple juice
1/4 cup whipping cream

Melt butter in a large skillet over medium-high heat. Add carrots and apple juice. Cover and cook until carrots are just tender-crisp, about 5 to 10 minutes, stirring frequently.

Stirring constantly, add cream and cook uncovered until most of the liquid has evaporated and carrots are glazed. Serve immediately.

GRILLED ZUCCHINI WITH ROSEMARY

This is an excellent way to use up your summer zucchini harvest.

6 medium zucchini
¼ cup olive oil
1 tbs. fresh rosemary, minced, or 1 tsp. dried
½ tsp. salt

Prepare a hot grill. Trim ends from zucchinis and slice lengthwise into ¼-inch slices. In a small bowl, combine olive oil, rosemary and salt. Brush one side of each slice with some of the olive oil mixture.

Place slices oil-side down on the hot grill. Brush remaining sides with remaining oil. Grill for about 3 minutes, turn and cook until tender, about 3 to 4 more minutes. Remove to a warm serving dish and serve.

SAUTÉED SPINACH WITH PINE NUTS

Be sure to thoroughly wash your spinach to prevent any sand or grit in your final dish.

2 lb. fresh spinach
3 tbs. olive oil
2 cloves garlic, minced
$\frac{1}{2}$ tsp. salt
$\frac{1}{4}$ cup pine nuts

Remove stems from spinach and discard. In a large skillet, heat oil over medium-high heat. Add garlic and sauté until garlic begins to brown. Add spinach, salt and pine nuts and cook until spinach wilts, about 5 to 10 minutes. Remove to a warm serving platter and serve immediately.

Time-Saver Tip: Purchase packaged baby spinach leaves and save yourself the time it takes to thoroughly wash and rinse spinach purchased by the bunch.

SPINACH RICE ITALIANO

Most people think pasta when thinking of a starch side dish for an Italian entrée. Rice is a staple in Northern Italy, and this dish is a simple version of risotto.

3½ cups chicken broth
1 cup prepared tomato spaghetti sauce (such as Prego or Ragu)
1 pkg. (10 oz.) frozen chopped spinach, thawed and squeezed dry
2 cups long-grain white rice
½ tsp. salt

Heat oven to 375°. In a large covered casserole or other pot that can be used on the stovetop and in the oven, combine broth and spaghetti sauce. Bring mixture to a boil over high heat.

Remove from heat and stir in spinach, rice and salt. Stir well to mix. Cover and bake for 20 to 25 minutes. Remove from oven and let stand for 5 minutes prior to serving.

SWEET AND SOUR RED CABBAGE

Servings: 6-8

If you are oven-roasting pork ribs, try this as a spicy side dish.

1 head red cabbage
2 tbs. butter
2 yellow onions, sliced
2 Granny Smith apples, peeled and sliced
2 tbs. cider vinegar
2 tbs. brown sugar

Cut cabbage in half and remove core and tough white stems; slice cabbage into thin strips.

Melt butter in a large Dutch oven or stew pot over medium heat. Add onions and apples and sauté until onions are tender, about 10 minutes. Add cabbage, vinegar and brown sugar and stir to mix. Reduce heat to low and cover. Simmer for 15 minutes, stirring occasionally, until cabbage is tender.

VEGETABLE COUSCOUS

Couscous is very tiny, precooked pasta. The vegetable addition adds both moisture and flavor.

2 small zucchini
8 green onions
olive oil
1 1/2 cups chicken broth

2/3 cup uncooked couscous
2 tbs. butter
1/2 tsp. salt

Trim ends from zucchini and slice zucchini in half lengthwise. Trim ends from green onions. Lightly brush zucchini and green onions with olive oil. Place zucchini and green onions on a baking sheet and place under a hot broiler. Cook green onions until just beginning to char, about 3 minutes. Cook zucchini until tender-crisp, about 5 minutes on each side. Remove from oven and let cool slightly.

While vegetables are cooling, bring chicken broth to a boil in a medium saucepan over high heat. When boiling, remove from heat and add couscous, stirring to break up any lumps. Cover and let sit for 5 minutes.

Cut onions into 1/4-inch slices and coarsely chop zucchini. Add onions and zucchini to couscous with butter and salt. Stir to mix well and melt butter. Serve immediately.

POTATOES, RICE, PASTA AND BEANS

GARLIC-CRUSTED POTATOES

You can peel the potatoes if you prefer, but I like the color and texture the potato skins add.

2 lb. red or other thin-skinned potatoes
$1/4$ cup butter
2 tbs. olive oil
5 cloves garlic, minced

Place potatoes in a large pot and cover with water. (If potatoes are large, cut into large pieces to speed up cooking time.) Bring to a boil and reduce heat to medium-high. Cook until potatoes are tender, about 15 to 20 minutes, depending on size. Drain and set aside.

Heat butter and olive oil together in a large skillet over medium heat. Add garlic and stir to coat. Add potatoes, and using a spatula, press potatoes down, slightly mashing them. Do not stir! Let them cook for about 5 minutes, and then invert onto a plate. The golden garlic crust will be on top. Serve immediately.

MASHED POTATOES AND
CELERY ROOT WITH JARLSBERG

Plain mashed potatoes get a flavor and texture boost from the addition of celery root and tangy Jarlsberg cheese.

1 lb. thin-skinned potatoes, quartered, but not peeled
2 lb. celery root, peeled and cut into chunks
3 tbs. butter
1 tsp. salt
1 cup grated Jarlsberg cheese

Place potatoes and celery root in a large saucepan and cover with water. Bring to boil over high heat, reduce heat to medium and cook until potatoes and celery root are tender, about 20 minutes.

Preheat broiler. Drain potatoes and celery root and mash or beat with a mixer until almost smooth. Add butter and salt and stir to mix. Place mixture in a shallow pan. Sprinkle with grated cheese and place under broiler until cheese is melted and bubbly, about 5 minutes. Serve hot.

POTATO AND ARTICHOKE SAUTÉ

Servings: 4

You can use either frozen or canned artichoke hearts for this, but don't use the marinated ones!

3 tbs. olive oil
1 clove garlic, minced
1 lb. new potatoes, quartered
1 cup chicken broth
2 cups artichoke hearts
salt to taste

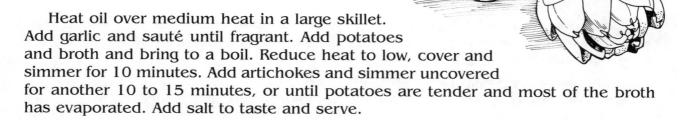

Heat oil over medium heat in a large skillet. Add garlic and sauté until fragrant. Add potatoes and broth and bring to a boil. Reduce heat to low, cover and simmer for 10 minutes. Add artichokes and simmer uncovered for another 10 to 15 minutes, or until potatoes are tender and most of the broth has evaporated. Add salt to taste and serve.

SKILLET POTATOES AND PEPPERS

Servings: 4

I enjoy serving this with a nice herb-roasted chicken and a glass of white wine. If the chicken broth is salty, you may wish to omit the added salt in the recipe.

3 tbs. olive oil
1 yellow onion, sliced
1 lb. new potatoes, quartered
1/2 cup chicken broth
1/2 tsp. salt
1 green bell pepper
1 red bell pepper

Heat oil over medium heat in a large skillet. Add onion and sauté until translucent. Add potatoes, broth and salt, and bring to a boil. Reduce heat to low, cover and simmer for 15 minutes.

Cut peppers in half and remove core and seeds. Cut each half into 4 pieces. Add peppers and simmer covered for another 5 to 10 minutes, or until potatoes are tender.

TWICE-COOKED CREAMER POTATOES

Servings: 4

Try to find the tiniest new potatoes, called "creamers," that you can locate. The texture is even finer with the smaller potatoes.

1 lb. new potatoes, about 1-inch diameter
water
¼ cup butter
½ tsp. salt

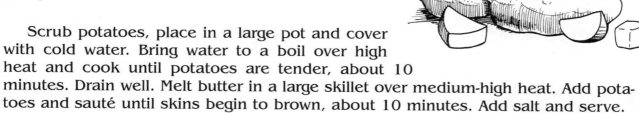

Scrub potatoes, place in a large pot and cover with cold water. Bring water to a boil over high heat and cook until potatoes are tender, about 10 minutes. Drain well. Melt butter in a large skillet over medium-high heat. Add potatoes and sauté until skins begin to brown, about 10 minutes. Add salt and serve.

Time-Saver Tip: Mix 1 tablespoon (or more, to taste) or dried herbs into 1¤2 cup softened butter for an instant herb spread for bread, or a tasty addition to baked potatoes or steamed vegetables.

WARM POTATO SALAD

Don't think of hot German potato salad, because this does not have a sweet-sour dressing, nor bacon. The Dijon and dill dressing add a spicy flavor to the creamy texture of white-skinned potatoes.

8 white skinned potatoes
2 eggs
1 tbs. Dijon mustard
1/2 cup olive oil
1 tsp. dried dill weed
1/3 cup cider vinegar

Place potatoes and eggs in a large pot and cover with water. Bring to a boil over high heat. Remove eggs after 10 minutes and continue to cook potatoes until they are just tender, but not soft, about 15 to 20 minutes.

While potatoes are cooking, combine mustard, olive oil, dill weed and vinegar. Set aside. Drain potatoes and eggs. Slice potatoes into 1/4-inch-thick slices. Place cut potatoes in a serving bowl. Thinly slice egg and place on top of potatoes. Pour dressing over all and gently toss to mix. Serve hot.

CHIPOTLE RICE

This is a southwestern-flavored rice that goes great with most grilled meats or poultry. It is fairly spicy, but if you really want fire, use 3 or 4 chipotle peppers. You'll usually find them with the other dried peppers in the Mexican foods section of your supermarket.

2 chipotle peppers, seeded and quartered
3 cups chicken broth
1 cup white rice
1/2 cup minced yellow onion
3 tbs. tomato paste
1/2 tsp. ground cumin
1 tsp. salt

In a medium saucepan, combine all ingredients. Bring mixture to a boil over high heat. Stir and reduce heat to low. Cover, stirring occasionally, and let cook for 20 minutes. Rice will be a bit "saucy," so don't continue to cook once the rice is tender.

RICE PILAF CHINESE-STYLE

This rice has the flavors of Chinese fried rice, but is prepared as a pilaf.

1/4 cup butter
1 cup long-grain white rice
1 can (14 1/2 oz.) chicken broth
1 tbs. soy sauce
3/4 cup fresh or frozen green peas
2 eggs, beaten
1/4 cup slivered green onions

In a medium saucepan, melt butter over high heat. Add rice, and stir to coat all grains. Cook on high, stirring constantly, until rice begins to brown, about 5 minutes. Add broth and soy sauce, and bring to a full boil. Reduce heat to low, cover and simmer for 15 minutes.

At the end of 15 minutes, add peas and stir to mix. Pour beaten egg over rice and cover (do not stir rice after adding egg). Simmer for an additional 5 minutes to cook egg. Remove from heat and stir to mix. Place in a warm serving bowl and sprinkle with slivered green onions.

RICE WITH ALMONDS

Servings: 4

This is a simple way to dress up white rice — it is very easy, and complements most seafood dishes.

2 cups water
1/2 tsp. salt
1 cup long-grain white rice
2 tbs. butter
1/2 cup slivered or sliced almonds

In a medium saucepan, bring water and salt to a boil over high heat. Add rice, cover and reduce heat to low. Cook until all water is absorbed, about 20 minutes.

While rice is cooking, in a small pan, melt butter over medium heat. Add almonds and sauté until light golden brown. Stir almonds and butter into cooked rice and serve.

Time-Saver Tip: Always keep shredded cheese on hand — you can use it to quickly dress up baked potatoes, stir it into hot rice or top your garlic bread.

SOUTHWEST RICE

Servings: 4

Cumin and garlic flavor the rice, and make this a perfect side dish for most grilled meats, poultry or fish.

2 tbs. olive oil
1 cup white rice
2-3 cloves garlic, minced
1 can (14½ oz.) chicken broth
¼ tsp. salt
¼ tsp. cayenne pepper
½ tsp. ground cumin

In a medium saucepan, heat oil over medium-high heat. Add rice and sauté until rice is just beginning to turn golden. Add garlic and continue to sauté until most rice is golden. Add chicken broth, salt, cayenne and cumin; stir to mix and bring to a boil. Reduce heat to low, cover and simmer for about 20 minutes, or until rice is done and broth has been absorbed.

SESAME NOODLES

Sesame oil is very strong, but has a wonderful flavor — these simple noodles make the perfect accompaniment to most spicy Asian entrées.

8 oz. uncooked angel hair pasta
1/4 cup butter
1 tbs. sesame oil
1/2 tsp. salt
1 tbs. sesame seeds

Cook pasta according to package directions. While pasta is cooking, melt butter in a small saucepan. Add sesame oil and salt, stir and set aside until pasta is cooked.

Pour butter mixture over cooked, drained pasta. Toss well to coat evenly. Sprinkle sesame seeds over pasta and toss. Serve immediately.

ORZO WITH PORCINI CREAM

Servings: 6-8

The earthy flavor of porcini mushrooms enhances bold entrées, such as game, beef and pork.

$^1/_2$ cup chicken broth
$^1/_2$ oz. dried porcini mushrooms
1 cup heavy cream
$^1/_2$ tsp. salt
12 oz. orzo
grated Parmesan cheese

Heat chicken broth to a full boil in a small saucepan. Add mushrooms, cover and simmer for 5 minutes. Remove mushrooms, reserving broth. Rinse mushrooms and chop finely. Strain both through a fine sieve, or line a sieve with cheesecloth. Discard solids and return broth and mushrooms to saucepan. Add cream and salt and bring to a boil, stirring frequently. Reduce heat to low and simmer for 10 minutes.

While sauce simmers, cook pasta according to package directions. Drain and place in a warm serving bowl. Pour sauce over pasta, toss to mix and serve immediately.

REFRIED BEANS AND SALSA

Servings: 4

This is an easy way to dress up canned refried beans. It makes a tasty side dish, and it's also good to serve as a dip with tortilla chips.

2 cans (16 oz. each) refried beans
1 cup shredded cheddar cheese
1 cup hot salsa or picante sauce
$\frac{1}{2}$ cup sour cream

Heat oven to 400°. Place beans in a 2-quart casserole dish and spread out evenly. Sprinkle cheese over beans and spoon salsa over cheese.

Bake until hot, about 20 minutes. Remove from oven and spoon sour cream on top in dollops. Serve immediately.

TEX MEX BLACK BEANS

This is a spicy update of baked beans. Use your favorite salsa or picante sauce — hot or mild, depending on the amount of heat you prefer.

2 cans (15 oz. each) black beans
1 cup salsa
1/3 cup brown sugar, packed
5 slices cooked bacon, crumbled
1/4 tsp. ground cumin

Heat oven to 425°. In a medium-sized ovenproof baking dish, combine all ingredients. Cover with a lid or cover tightly with aluminum foil, and bake for 25 minutes. Remove from oven and serve immediately.

DESSERTS

PEACH NECTAR ICE CREAM

Sweet peach nectar is pureed peaches, sugar and water. All you need to do to make a rich ice cream is add the cream and freeze.

1 can (12 oz.) peach nectar, chilled
½ cup heavy cream
½ cup chopped canned peaches

In a medium bowl, mix all ingredients. Place ingredients in your ice cream freezer, and process according to manufacturer's directions until firm, about 20 to 25 minutes. Serve immediately.

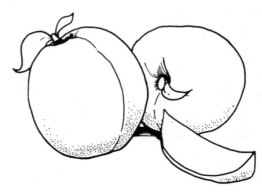

CANTALOUPE ICE

This is so easy, it is almost embarrassing. But it tastes so good after a spicy meal that I had to include it.

2 very ripe cantaloupes
1/2 cup sugar
1/2 cup strawberries, washed and hulled

Peel and seed cantaloupes. Cut into small chunks and place in a blender container in batches. Pulse to puree melon. Transfer pureed cantaloupe to a large bowl, and continue until all cantaloupe has been pureed. Add sugar and strawberries to blender container and pulse to puree. Add strawberry-sugar mixture to puréed cantaloupe. Stir to mix. Pour into an ice cream maker, and freeze according to manufacturer's directions. Remove from freezer bowl when very thick and serve.

COFFEE GRANITA

A cross between an ice cream and an ice, this is wonderful on a hot summer evening. It should be frozen only enough to be slushy, not firm.

2 cups strong coffee, chilled
1½ cups sugar
1 cup heavy cream
1 tsp. vanilla extract

Combine all ingredients in a medium bowl. Pour into a ice cream maker, according to manufacturer's directions. Freeze until thick and slushy. Serve at once.

HOT LEMON SAUCE

This hot sauce can be used on most plain cakes or poached fruits. You can also make this an orange sauce by substituting orange juice and zest for the lemon juice and zest.

$3/4$ cup plus 2 tbs. water, divided
$1/4$ tsp. salt
$1/4$ cup sugar
juice of 1 lemon
1 tbs. cornstarch
1 tbs. butter
zest of 1 lemon, grated

In a small saucepan, combine $3/4$ cup water, salt, sugar and lemon juice. Bring to boil over high heat. In a small bowl, mix together 2 tbs. water and cornstarch, and stir until smooth. Stirring constantly, add dissolved cornstarch to boiling mixture. Return to a boil and immediately remove from heat. Add butter and zest and stir until butter has completely melted. You can store this sauce in the refrigerator for about 1 week.

BERRY SAUCE

The wonderful thing about fruit sauces is that you can use fresh or frozen fruit, both with perfect results. The addition of Grand Marnier enhances the sauce, but can be omitted if desired. Try this over poached pears for a stunning dessert.

2 cups strawberries, raspberries, blackberries or any combination
1/2 cup granulated sugar
1/3 cup water
1/4 cup Grand Marnier liqueur

In a medium saucepan, combine berries, sugar and water. Bring mixture to a boil, stirring frequently, until berries begin to break down, about 3 minutes. Remove from heat and stir in the Grand Marnier. Serve warm or cold. You can store this sauce in the refrigerator for about 4 days.

BITTERSWEET CHOCOLATE SAUCE

A good chocolate sauce can instantly create a satisfying dessert — use it to top cakes, ice cream, poached fruit, or even custards and soufflés.

4 oz. bittersweet chocolate
1/2 cup brewed coffee or espresso
1 1/2 cups half-and-half
1/2 tsp. salt
1 tsp. vanilla extract

In a medium saucepan, melt chocolate in coffee over medium-low heat. Add half-and-half and stir until thickened and well blended, about 5 minutes. Remove from heat and add salt and vanilla. Serve warm or cold. You can store this sauce in the refrigerator for about 1 week.

CHOCOLATE AMARETTO FONDUE

The amaretto liqueur in this fondue compliments most fruits and cakes. You can omit the amaretto if you prefer a nonalcoholic version.

1 lb. semisweet chocolate, chopped
1 cup heavy cream
$\frac{1}{4}$ cup amaretto
pound cake, cut into cubes
fresh strawberries
fresh banana slices
fresh pear slices
fresh raspberries

In a medium saucepan, combine chocolate and cream. Heat over low heat, stirring very frequently, until chocolate has completely melted and mixture is smooth. Remove from heat and add amaretto. Stir to mix. If desired, transfer to a fondue pot and keep warm over a heat source. Serve with cake pieces and fresh fruit.

VANILLA RUM CUSTARD

This custard is very light, a cross between a soufflé and a standard custard, and should be served hot from the oven. Serve with Bittersweet Chocolate Sauce, page 106, for a very elegant dessert.

4 eggs
1 1/2 cups milk
1/4 cup light rum
1/2 cup sugar
1 tsp. vanilla extract

Heat oven to 350°. Prepare a 2-quart casserole dish by spraying bottom and sides with nonstick spray.

In a large bowl, using an electric mixer on medium speed, beat eggs until light, about 3 minutes. Add remaining ingredients and mix on high speed for 1 minute. Pour mixture into prepared dish. Bake uncovered for 25 minutes. Serve immediately.

LEMON RICOTTA CUPS

Cheese is the usual final course in Italian meals — here you have the cheese, sweetened with sugar and lemon zest.

1 lb. ricotta cheese
$1/2$ cup light cream
1 tbs. grated lemon zest
$1/2$ cup sugar
$1/2$ cup graham cracker crumbs

In a large bowl, combine ricotta, cream, lemon zest and sugar. Using a mixer, beat on medium speed until well blended and light. Sprinkle graham cracker crumbs in the bottom of 4 to 6 individual ramekins or small bowls. Scoop ricotta mixture into bowls. Cover with plastic wrap and refrigerate for 15 minutes before serving.

PAPAYA FOSTER

This dessert works well with most tropical fruits — the traditional banana, mango or even pineapple.

1/2 cup butter
1/2 cup honey
2 large papayas
1/4 cup rum
1/4 cup flaked coconut

In a medium saucepan over medium heat, combine butter and honey. Heat until butter has melted and incorporated with honey.

Peel and seed papaya. Cut into thick slices, about 1/2-inch thick. Add to butter-honey mixture and heat until papaya is warmed through, about 5 minutes. Add rum, and using a long wooden match, ignite sauce. It will flame only for a moment, but enough to burn off the alcohol.

Spoon papayas and sauce into warm serving dishes and top with flaked coconut. Serve hot.

PEACHES WITH CHAMPAGNE SAUCE

Servings: 6

This is a really elegant way to serve fresh, sweet peaches.

3 cups water
1½ cups sugar, divided
1 tsp. vanilla extract
3 large peaches, peeled, halved and pitted
6 egg yolks
1 cup champagne
French vanilla ice cream

In a large pot, mix together water, 1 cup sugar and vanilla, and bring to a boil over high heat. Reduce heat to low and add peaches. Simmer uncovered for 10 minutes, or until peaches are tender and glazed. Remove peaches from water and cool. Discard water.

While peaches are cooking, prepare sauce. In a small saucepan, combine egg yolks and ½ cup sugar. Cook over low heat until mixture coats the back of a spoon. Add champagne slowly, beating well. Continue to cook until mixture is thickened. Place a peach on a serving plate with a scoop of ice cream next to it. Top with champagne sauce.

PEARS WITH CINNAMON SAUCE

Servings: 4

If you are using your oven for your meal, you can bake this dessert as you take your dish out — it will be ready when you are.

2 Bartlett pears, halved and peeled
1 ½ tsp. ground cinnamon
¼ cup butter, melted
½ cup brown sugar, packed
¼ cup brandy or rum

Heat oven to 350°. Core pears and place them cut-side down in an 8-inch buttered baking dish. In a small bowl, mix together cinnamon, butter and brown sugar. Rub cinnamon paste over each of pears, using all paste. Bake for 20 minutes. Remove dish from oven, pour brandy over pears and return to oven. Bake for an additional 5 to 10 minutes, or until pears are tender. Serve warm with sauce.

APPLE BLACKBERRY CRISP

You can assemble this while your dinner is cooking, and then bake it while you have dinner, for a perfectly timed hot dessert.

$^1/_4$ cup flour
$^1/_4$ cup uncooked oatmeal
$^1/_4$ cup brown sugar
$^1/_4$ cup butter
3 large Granny Smith apples, thinly sliced
2 cups blackberries, defrosted if frozen
2 tbs. granulated sugar
1 tbs. cornstarch

Heat oven to 400°. Prepare an 8-inch square baking dish by spraying the bottom and sides with nonstick spray. Prepare topping: In a small bowl, combine flour, oats, brown sugar and butter with your fingers until crumbly. Set aside. In a medium bowl, combine apples, blackberries, sugar and cornstarch. Gently toss until apples and blackberries are fully coated with cornstarch and sugar. Transfer apple-blackberry mixture to prepared pan. Top with crisp topping mixture. Bake for 25 minutes. Remove from oven and let cool slightly. Serve warm, or refrigerate until cold.

RUM RAISIN BREAD PUDDING

Servings: 4

This is richly flavored comfort food, and can be done very fast. Try to use stale bread if possible — it makes a firmer texture.

4 slices bread
$1/_3$ cup light rum
$1/_2$ cup sugar
3 eggs
2 cups milk
$1/_2$ tsp. salt
1 tsp. vanilla extract
$1/_2$ cup raisins

Heat oven to 425°. Butter bottom and sides of four 2-cup ramekins.

Into each ramekin, tear 1 slice of bread into small pieces. In a medium bowl, combine rum, sugar, eggs, milk, salt and vanilla, and stir well to mix. Pour an equal amount over bread in each ramekin. Top each ramekin with approximately 2 tbs. raisins. Bake ramekins for 20 minutes, or until a knife inserted in the center comes out clean. Serve immediately.

POUND CAKE WITH LEMON CREAM CHEESE FROSTING AND BLACKBERRIES

Servings: 8-10

A really beautiful dessert, and dramatic enough for parties and guests.

1 pound cake, 16 oz.
8 oz. cream cheese
2 tsp. grated lemon zest
2½ cups confectioners' sugar
16 oz. fresh blackberries

Slice pound cake horizontally into 4 layers. Set aside.

In a medium bowl, use an electric mixer to beat cream cheese and lemon zest just until blended. Add confectioners' sugar, 1 cup at a time, and beat until smooth enough to spread.

Place a layer of the pound cake on a serving platter. Spread ⅓ of the frosting on top of layer. Continue with other layers, ending with a layer unfrosted on top.

Slice cake vertically, and place a few blackberries on each slice.

GINGER SPICE CAKE

This is an old-fashioned gingerbread-style cake — it can be frosted with a cream cheese frosting, or served with Hot Lemon Sauce, *page 104.*

³/₄ cup hot water
1 cup molasses
¹/₂ cup brown sugar, packed
1 tsp. ground ginger
1 tsp. cinnamon
¹/₂ tsp. nutmeg
¹/₂ tsp. ground cloves
¹/₂ cup butter, melted
2 eggs, beaten
2¹/₂ cups sifted all-purpose flour
¹/₂ tsp. salt
2 tsp. baking powder
¹/₂ tsp. baking soda

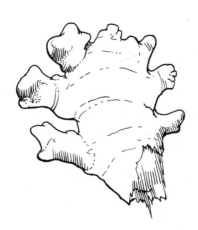

Heat oven to 350°. Butter the bottom and sides of an 8-inch square baking dish.

In a large bowl, mix together hot water, molasses and brown sugar. Stir in ginger, cinnamon, nutmeg, cloves and melted butter. Stir in eggs and mix well.

In another bowl, stir together flour, salt, baking powder and baking soda. Add flour mixture to wet ingredients and mix thoroughly. Pour batter into prepared dish and bake for 20 to 25 minutes. Let cool slightly before cutting into squares.

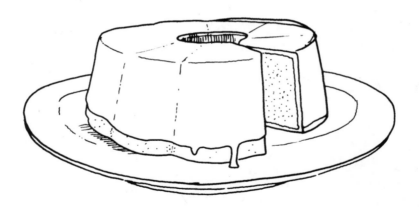

INDEX

A

Amaretto chocolate fondue 107
Angel hair pasta with sun-dried
    tomatoes 73
Apple(s)
    and avocado salad with
      chicken 12
    blackberry crisp 113
    chicken with 39
Artichoke and tomato sauce pasta
    72
Artichoke and potato sauté 88
Asian chicken salad, spicy 14
Asparagus with red pepper butter
    76
Avocado and apple salad with
    chicken 12

B

Bean(s)
    black, soup 4
    black, Tex Mex 99
    black, wings, Asian 36
    Mexican salad 17
    refried and salsa 98

    soup, Italian 3
    white, and pancetta salad 10
Bean sprouts, cold sauced 78
Beef
    fajita-style stir-fry 52
    garlicky steaks 51
    grilled rib-eye steaks 53
    rustic meat and vegetable
      pasta 62
    salad, cold 18
    steaks with green peppercorn
      sauce 63
    velvet 64
Berry sauce 105
Blackberries and pound cake with
    cream cheese frosting 115
Blackberry apple crisp 113
Bread pudding, rum raisin 114

C

Cabbage, red, sweet and sour 83
Cajun prawns 23
Cake
    ginger spice 116

    pound, with lemon cream
      cheese frosting and black-
      berries 115
Cantaloupe ice 102
Carrot and squash soup 6
Carrots, cream-glazed 79
Celery root and potatoes mashed
    with Jarlsberg 87
Champagne sauce, peaches with 111
Cheddar chile fondue 70
Chicken
    in apple and avocado salad 12
    with apples 39
    breasts, Sicilian-style stuffed
      45
    country French 46
    with Italian sausage and
      peppers 40
    lemon 41
    Pacific Rim 42
    pecan salad 16
    with pepper cream 33
    red curry 47
    red-sauced 43
    in red wine 38
    salad, spicy Asian 14

Serve Creative, Easy, Nutritious Meals with Nitty Gritty® Cookbooks

100 Dynamite Desserts
The 9 x 13 Pan Cookbook
Beer and Good Food
The Best Bagels are Made at Home
The Best Pizza is Made at Home
Bread Baking
Bread Machine Cookbook
Bread Machine Cookbook II
Bread Machine Cookbook III
Bread Machine Cookbook IV
Bread Machine Cookbook V
Bread Machine Cookbook VI
Cappuccino/Espresso
Casseroles
The Coffee Book
Convection Oven Cookery
Cooking for 1 or 2
Cooking in Clay
Cooking in Porcelain
Cooking with Chile Peppers
Cooking with Grains
Cooking with Parchment
Cooking with Your Kids *(new)*
Creative Mexican Cooking
Deep Fried Indulgences

The Dehydrator Cookbook
Easy Vegetarian Cooking
Edible Pockets for Every Meal
Entrées From your Bread Machine
Extra-Special Crockery Pot
Fabulous Fiber Cookery
Fondue and Hot Dips *(new)*
Fresh Vegetables
From Freezer, 'Fridge, and Pantry
From Your Ice Cream Maker
The Garlic Cookbook *(new)*
Gourmet Gifts
Healthy Cooking on the Run
Healthy Snacks for Kids
Indoor Grilling
The Juicer Book
The Juicer Book II
Lowfat American Favorites
Marinades
Muffins and Nut Breads
The New Blender Book
New International Fondue Cookbook
No Salt, No Sugar, No Fat
One Dish Meals
Oven and Rotisserie Roasting

Party Fare
The Pasta Machine Cookbook
Pinch of Time: Meals in Less than 30
   Minutes *(new)*
Quick and Easy Pasta Recipes
Recipes for the Loaf Pan
Recipes for your Pressure Cooker
Recipes for Yogurt Cheese
Risottos, Paellas, and other Rice
Specialties
The Sandwich Maker Cookbook
Sautés
Slow Cooking in Crock Pot, Slow Cooker,
   Oven and Multi-Cooker *(new)*
The Steamer Cookbook
The Toaster Oven Cookbook
Unbeatable Chicken Recipes
The Versatile Rice Cooker
Waffles
The Well Dressed Potato
The Wok
Worldwide Sourdoughs from Your
   Bread Machine
Wraps and Roll-Ups

For a free catalog, write or call: Bristol Publishing Enterprises, Inc.
P.O. Box 1737,
San Leandro, California 94577
(800) 346-4889
(510) 895-4461